BIRDS

Amazon Parrots

James E. Gerholdt
ABDO & Daughters

Published by Abdo & Daughters, 4940 Viking Drive, Suite 622, Edina, Minnesota 55435.

Printed in the United States.

Cover and Interior Photo credits: Peter Arnold, Inc.

Edited by Julie Berg

Library of Congress Cataloging-in-Publication Data

Gerholdt, James E., 1943—
     Amazon Parrots/James E. Gerholdt.
         p.   cm. -- (birds)
     Includes index.
     Summary: Describes the physical characteristics, habits, and natural habitat of these birds that are popular as pets because of their bright colors and ability to learn tricks.
     ISBN 1-56239-587-4
     1. Amazon parrots--Juvenile literature. [1. Amazon parrots. 2. Parrots.] I. Title. II. Series: Gerholdt, James E., 1943—Birds.
     QL696.P7G47   1997
     598.7'1--dc20   96-708
                                                            CIP
                                                            AC

Contents

AMAZON PARROTS

Amazon parrots belong to one of the 28 **orders** of **birds**. They are in the same **family** as macaws, cockatoos, parakeets, and lorikeets. There are about 27 types of Amazon parrots in the world.

Birds are **vertebrates**. This means they have backbones, just like humans. And like humans, birds are **warm-blooded**.

These brightly-colored birds are very popular pets because they can repeat words and learn tricks. Some types of Amazon parrots are now **endangered**, partly because they are taken from their nests and sold.

Opposite page: A red-lored Amazon parrot.

SIZES

Amazon parrots are medium to large-size **birds**. The females and the males are often the same size. Sometimes the males are larger.

The different types weigh from as little as 6 3/4 ounces (190g) to more than 20 ounces (565g). From the tip of the beak to the tip of the tail, they measure 9 to 18 inches (23 to 45 cm). The **wingspan** is about twice the length of the body.

Opposite page: A red-crowned Amazon parrot, an endangered species of Brazil.

SHAPES

Amazon parrots are round-bodied and **stocky**. Their tails are short and slightly rounded. The heavy beak is strong and has a notch in the upper part. It curves down and is pointed at the tip.

The head is large and the neck is short. Amazon parrots' wings are broad and rounded. These **birds** have strong feet so they can **perch** on a tree branch. They grab with two toes in front and two toes in back.

Opposite page: The Amazon parrot has strong feet that when perched on a branch grab and hold tightly.

COLORS

One thing people like about Amazon parrots is their bright colors. Both males and females have the same colors.

The basic body color is bright green. But the St. Vincent Amazon is often an orange-brown color. Other types have red, yellow, blue, and purple colors on their head, wings, and tail.

Opposite page: This red-browed Amazon parrot is very colorful.

WHERE THEY LIVE

All Amazon parrots live in the **New World**. None are found in the United States. Most types are found in South America. But others are found as far north as Mexico. The St. Vincent Amazon and the St. Lucia Amazon are two types found only on certain islands.

Some of the Amazon parrots like dry areas, but most live in the forest. Cutting down these forests takes away their survival in the modern world.

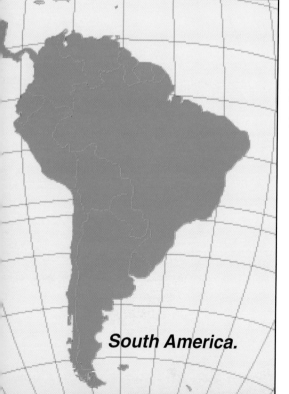

South America.

Opposite page: Blue-fronted Amazon parrot.

12

SENSES

Amazon parrots are one of the smartest types of **birds**. They have the same five senses as humans. Their senses of taste and smell are better than most birds. As pets they often develop a liking for special treats.

Like other kinds of birds, their vision and hearing are very good. They are also very noisy. Amazon parrots can learn to repeat sounds and words. But they can't really talk with you.

Opposite page: A white-fronted Amazon parrot. They have very good eyesight.

DEFENSE

Many different **predators** eat Amazon parrots. But an important defense against these enemies is their color. Amazon parrots live in the forests, so their bright green colors blend in with the plants and trees. This is called **camouflage**.

If an enemy does find them, they can fly away to safety. Their strong beaks can also bite hard if they are attacked.

The most dangerous enemy to the Amazon parrots are humans, who sell the parrots and cut down their forest homes.

Opposite page: The green color of the parrot helps it to blend in with its surroundings and its sharp beak and claws help to defend itself.

FOOD

Amazon parrots eat many kinds of foods. Their strong beaks can crack open hard nut shells so the insides can be eaten. The food is held with one foot while the **bird** eats. Amazon parrots also eat fruits, berries, seeds, and flowers.

Sometimes Amazon parrots find food in farm fields. In **captivity**, Amazon parrots have favorite foods. They like bones with a little meat left on them.

Opposite page: This Amazon parrot is feeding on arassa fruits.

BABIES

Amazon parrots hatch from eggs. The eggs are small to medium-sized, and are 1.2 by .9 inches (30 by 22.7mm) to 1 3/4 by 1 1/2 inches (44.5 by 38mm).

The nest is built in a tree hole high above the ground. Sometimes the **birds** use the old nesting hole of a woodpecker. One to five eggs are laid and hatched in 28 days. The young leave the nest when they are around two months old.

Opposite page: Shown are various stages of a baby parrot, starting with an egg, then 3, 5, 22, and 40 days old.

GLOSSARY

bird (BURD) - A feathered animal with a backbone whose front limbs are wings.

camouflage (CAM-a-flaj) - The ability to blend in with the surroundings.

captivity (kap-TIV-uh-tee) - The condition of being held against one's will.

endangered - Almost extinct.

family (FAM-i-lee) - A grouping of animals.

New World - North America and South America.

order (OAR-der) - A grouping of animals, ranking above the family.

perch - Anything on which a bird can come to rest, such as a bar or branch. Also, to sit.

predator (PRED-a-tore) - An animal that eats other animals.

species (SPEE-seas) - A kind or type.

stocky - Having a solid or sturdy body.

vertebrate (VER-tuh-brit) - An animal with a backbone.

warm-blooded (warm-BLUD-ed) - Regulating body temperature at a constant level, from inside the body.

wingspan - The distance from one wing tip to the other.

INDEX